HOME
AWAY FROM
HOME

**Turning Your International Relocation
Into A Lifetime Enhancement**

By Beverly D. Roman

Published by BR Anchor Publishing

ISBN 1-888891-18-1

Edited by Dalene R. Bickel

Cover and book design by Michael J. Cadieux. Michael is an award-winning graphics designer and an accomplished illustrator. His creative art has been published in many books and displayed in national advertisement campaigns.

Home Away From Home is distributed by:
BR Anchor Publishing, 2044 Montrose Lane, Wilmington, NC 28405
Tel: (910) 256-9598, In the United States, (800) 727-7691
Fax: (910) 256-9579
E-mail: branchor@inttek.net
Visit BR Anchor Publishing on the Web: http://www.branchor.com

Printed in Canada

Joy Loverde, author of THE COMPLETE ELDERCARE PLANNER, (Hyperion) offers advice on pages 31 and 32. Her book is an excellent resource for families with elder care responsibilities. Written with the time-taxed reader in mind, it includes checklists, action plans, The Documents Locator, record-keeping forms, questions to ask and more. Joy Loverde is a professional speaker on elder care-related topics.
E-mail: jloverde@elderindustry.com or Silvercare Productions
(312) 642-3611. On the web: http://www.elderindustry.com

INTRODUCTION

In a 1998 survey titled "Measuring Expatriate Success," conducted by *Workforce* magazine in conjunction with Prudential Relocation International, it was stated: "Many assignees are sent abroad without clearly defined goals for the assignment and the repatriation process is rocky at best."

Having experienced 18 moves, domestically and internationally, I firmly believe the level of overall success a family can achieve is directly proportionate to the preparation and information they receive prior to an assignment. Living and working in another country should be all it is meant to be—a unique personal and professional experience. Every relocation should become an opportunity for the entire family. This book is designed to help you achieve these goals.

Home Away From Home will give you an overall representation of what you need to do to prepare for and enjoy your international move. Its proven international relocation advice, valuable checklists, business card sleeves and handy pouches are all designed to help you organize your move and smooth your transition to another country.

And—just for fun! See if you can guess which countries pertain to the customs described on various pages throughout the book. The answers appear on page 110.

HOME
AWAY FROM
HOME

CONTENTS

EVALUATION

Relocating abroad involves lifestyle and cultural changes, as well as varied work ethics and attitudes. Before you make a commitment to the assignment, understand these aspects about the country and evaluate everything that is important to you and your family. Children's ages and activities, the length of the overseas tour, your spouse's career and possibly elder care responsibilities will all impact your decision.

Evaluate your own personal and professional goals, as well as those of your spouse. Employees need to know how the assignment is applicable to their career plans and how it will fit into the corporate business structure after repatriation. Spouses have to evaluate how the disruption or termination of their job will affect their careers and how this will impact the family. You should also feel comfortable with answers to questions such as:

❐ Are you adventuresome?

❐ Do you take yourself too seriously?

❐ Can you laugh at yourself?

❐ Do you feel uncomfortable in unfamiliar situations?

❐ Do you make friends easily?

❐ Could you adapt to a different standard of living?

❐ Do you adjust to new situations easily?

❐ When complications arise, are you courteous and polite?

PRESENTING THE MOVE

When you have made the decision to relocate, the very next detail is to present the move to your family. This should be done in a unified and positive way, as appropriate for each child's age. Before doing so, try to anticipate questions or concerns that your children might have, as well as resolutions for the situations.

Many times relocation takes place during the summer months when school is not in session. However, don't be too concerned

11

if you are asked to move during the school year. This time frame can actually be more attractive. Moving in June for instance can mean a long summer without established friends, whereas moving during the school year will allow children to become involved with other children and activities more quickly.

ASSIGNMENT PLANNING

Preparation and information are the key ingredients in planning a move, the importance of which cannot be overstated. Learn as much as possible about your assignment and the destination country before you move, and you will eliminate a lot of surprises and disappointments. For instance, if the country has extreme temperatures, it will impact your decisions about what to pack and what to store. Heavy clothing could be totally useless, and precious family heirlooms could be damaged instead of safely stored in your home country. Your corporate relocation manager, the information in this book and a pre-move visit to the country will help you to evaluate significant details.

COUNTRY-SPECIFICS TO UNDERSTAND:

- customs, manners and culture
- importation laws
- medical care and insurance coverage
- safety factors
- immigration regulations
- currency exchange
- education/language instruction
- driving laws
- financial reimbursement and tax considerations
- housing options

NECESSARY DOCUMENTS

Work permits are required to obtain a job in another country. These will be provided by the transferee's employer; however, any spouse who wishes to work abroad will need to acquire his or her own. Documents such as visas, immunization and medical records, birth or marriage certificates, divorce decrees and international driving permits (renew if any will expire while you are abroad) may also be required. For country-specific information, as well as import restrictions and foreign currency, contact the consulate or embassy of your destination country. In the United States, you can call (202) 555-1212 to request direct telephone numbers. Visas are available from the Office of Immigration (703) 661-5100 or the Department of State (202) 647-0518. Also look into absentee voting procedures and forms. Important documents, i.e., passport, visa, social security card and permits should be copied before you move. Store one copy and carry another separately from the original documents.

PASSPORTS

For the most recent passport information, your best resources are the Embassies or consular offices for your country. Check on your options before you move in case a passport will need to be updated while you are abroad. If you will be living in a relatively small country, or a remote area that does not have an Embassy or consular office, you probably will have to travel to a neighboring country. To obtain a passport, you will need one or more of the following:

❑ a passport application

❑ proof of citizenship or a previous passport

❑ two recent identical passport-sized photographs

❑ the current fee

❑ proof of identity, i.e., driver's license, Social Security card or Birth Certificate

Information about passports for United States citizens can also be found under "Passport Agency" in the Yellow Pages or the Government Blue Pages of US telephone directories. In the US, passports are available from

▦ the American Automobile Association (AAA)

▦ government offices, which are listed at county courthouses

▦ designated post offices

▦ some travel agencies

Report loss of passports to a United States Embassy or write: Passport Services, 1425 K Street, NW, Washington, DC 20524. *See also* "The Embassy Web" on page 103.

SURFING THE WEB 101

If you are an Internet novice, you will be delighted to learn that "surfing the web" is actually very simple. Vast amounts of information on virtually every topic conceivable are available on the World Wide Web. Here are four steps to get you started.

1. Log-on to your Internet server which might be America Online, Juno, Netscape or Microsoft Internet Explorer;
2. Click on the button that says "Search" (normally at the top of the computer screen);
3. Select a search engine such as Yahoo, InfoSeek, Excite or AOL NetFind;
4. Type in a keyword of what you would like more information about (i.e., France). For the best results, use the suggested search tips.

When accessing the Internet to learn about your destination country, try to be as specific as possible about what you want to discover. A broad request such as "France" will bring up literally thousands of links to web sites about that country. "Narrow" your search by using additional keywords until you receive a manageable number of links about your desired topic (Example: Type "Paris, France" to learn about the entire city or type "Eiffel Tower" to learn about that architectural structure). You will also find numerous web sites listed in the "Directory of Internet Sites" on page 101.

INTERNATIONAL RESOURCES

- For information about Chambers of Commerce other than the US., call (202) 659-6000.
- General Federation of Women's Clubs maintains overseas organizations (202) 347-3168. These organizations have a multitude of services and publications to assist expatriates.

REAL ESTATE

The two most important points to smart home sales are showing a home to perfection and pricing it right for the market, i.e., current home sale ranges, neighborhood comparisons, the home's location, its condition and the time of year. To help you analyze your home for resale, look for a qualified estate agent.

SELECTING AN ESTATE AGENT

Look for representatives who are pursuing sales, returning telephone calls, aggressively working in their clients' best interest and whose only job is real estate. Your agent should be familiar with home sales in your price range and in comparable neighborhoods. Ask specifics about the agent's credentials, licensing and areas of expertise.

SELECTION CHECKLIST

☐ Ask for two or three satisfied clients (with comparable properties). Qualify all references.

☐ Ask what percentage of the asking price, on average, agents received for the homes they sold during the previous year.

☐ Request the average number of days their listed homes stayed on the market.

☐ Find out what types of homes the agents typically sell.

☐ Ask for a written advertising plan for your property with details such as, where, what and how often, as well as on-going marketing efforts. Discuss success of previous efforts.

☐ Establish a day (preferably Monday) for "feedback" of progress so you know about the activity, even if it's minimal.

☐ Ask "Why should I pick you over all other agents?"

When you feel comfortable with your choice of agent, arm this person with facts about your home, noting attributes that distinguish it from others in the neighborhood.

15

FACTS A REALTOR NEEDS TO KNOW

☐ maintenance records and warranties

☐ descriptive features of your home, property and neighborhood

☐ area schools, public transportation and churches

☐ your annual property taxes

☐ the history of services and contracts to your home

☐ all repairs or renovations that were completed within your home, especially those that have long-term benefits

☐ costs that are required to maintain your home, i.e., gas, electricity, heat and water bills

HOME SALES

OUTSIDE CHECKLIST ... THE FIRST IMAGE THE BUYERS SEE

☐ Prune and trim lawns, shrubs and trees.

☐ Plant flowers in appropriate areas to enhance your property, especially at the front entryway.

☐ Clean, repair and paint the mailbox, front door and window ledges.

☐ Organize all toys and equipment.

☐ Remove unsightly rubbish.

☐ Check that outside features, i.e., faucets, latches and garage doors, are in good working order.

☐ Be sure the house numbers are visible and easy to read.

INSIDE CHECKLIST ... IT NEEDS TO SHOUT WELCOME!

☐ Create a fresh clean smell (no tobacco or pet odors).

☐ Place fresh linens in bathrooms.

☐ Clean windows, walls and woodwork.

☐ Organize closets, storage areas and counters.

☐ Clean and vacuum floors and carpets.

☐ Clean all appliances that will remain in the home.

☐ Check all hardware and systems that will remain in the home to be sure they are in good working order, i.e., door hinges, faucets, knobs, appliances, heating system and fans.

☐ Vacate your home during prospective clients' appointments.

A FEW FINAL TIPS

⊞ Experts consider landscaping a 200 percent return on investment.

⊞ If you need to install a new heating system, consider a heat pump which will reduce heating and insurance costs.

⊞ The average homebuyer spends approximately 20 to 30 minutes viewing a home before seriously considering a purchase. Take extra steps to make every minute of a home showing count!

VACANT HOMES

If you move before your home is sold, obtain appropriate insurance and arrange for the home to appear occupied.

TIPS TO GIVE A HOME AN OCCUPIED APPEARANCE ARE:

❐ well-maintained exterior and interior, such as lawn and shrub care and snow removal;

❐ a reasonable temperature inside (extend electrical service);

❐ inside and outside illumination; (borrow lamps from a neighbor and place these on electrical timers);

❐ automatic devices (such as an attic fan) turned to the off position;

❐ drawn and closed drapery and shades.

Note: Ask a friend to periodically check on your home, but make arrangements in person or by telephone. Leaving messages outside indicates that no one is at home.

OVERSEAS HOUSING

Buying a home in a foreign country has limitations, and may be impossible if you are not a citizen of the country. Most companies do not encourage buying a home in foreign countries due to tax and real estate complications and currency risks. Begin by understanding your corporation's international relocation policy.

Write down what your family requires in household goods and living accommodations. Consider the amount of furniture and appliances you believe you will need, and how long your family could feasibly be living abroad. You may be encouraged by your employer to purchase or rent household goods abroad and store your belongings until your return. In some countries, household items can be economically purchased from expatriates who are moving on. Personnel at your company's foreign office will most likely be aware of how to contact other expats.

Before your pre-move visit to your new country, establish yourself with an estate agent or a reliable firm. You can ask expatriates who are living in the area to recommend agents and firms and you can also research the housing market on the Internet.

See also "Real Estate" on page 101 to locate Internet resources that will help you locate estate agents, homes and rentals and in-depth housing details for almost any country in the world.

> *In this country you should be prepared for a great deal of bargaining when making a purchase.*

RELOCATION INSURANCE

Relocation is an ideal time to evaluate and update your insurance policies. Begin by creating an inventory of your personal belongings and document them with photographs or a narrated descriptive home video. Moving companies also inventory household goods, but the contents are not always specific. For instance, a box could be marked "Dining room china" without noting the number of place settings.

See also "Personal Inventory" on pages 77 to 79.

CORPORATE POLICY

International moving insurance should be outlined for you by your corporate relocation department. If you want to supplement your company's coverage, you can do so through the moving company or from your own insurance agent. Specifically request "Replacement Cost Insurance" which will cover household goods for their current replacement value. Medical coverage needs to be reviewed with the company officer as well. You want to assure that you will have the same comprehensive insurance in the foreign country that you now enjoy at home. Also...

- know whether your insurance is applicable in the new country,
- find out if your insurance rates will change when you move,
- give your insurance agent your new address and move dates,
- check with your agent about the guidelines for vacant homes if you move before your home is sold.

WHAT SHOULD I MOVE?

A complete inventory will help you to obtain comprehensive insurance. The amount and type of personal goods that you decide to ship should be determined by their value and condition, the varying temperatures of the ship and the climate of your destination country. If you have items that you consider irreplaceable, you can entrust them to a friend, put them in storage or place them in a safety deposit box until you return. Consider that many over-the-water shipment policies exclude jewelry, stocks, bonds and stamp/coin collections.

Moving company personnel will provide the most current information about the items that are prohibited in your destination country. Flammable or hazardous materials can never be shipped with household goods.

COLLECTIBLES AND ANTIQUES

You will need documentation for high-priced collectibles such as antiques, art, jewelry, furs, silver and china. The original receipt and/or a current appraisal from the correct source, such as an antique dealer for antiques, will serve as authentic documentation. You can then obtain an insurance floater or have a rider policy for high value items. Carry these valuations with you when you move. The records, appraisals and video documentation will provide excellent proof of ownership and condition in case of damage to or loss of your belongings.

WHEN PACKING,

❑ secure furniture doors with soft cloth or large rubber bands;

❑ ask about having antiques, art or furniture placed in crates for the move abroad;

❑ tape furniture keys or loose pieces of furniture to the inside of a drawer, or place them in a labeled plastic bag;

❑ attach large notes on all items that require extra attention.

SHIPPING AUTOMOBILES

To ship a vehicle overseas, the owner is required to have at least three notarized copies of the car's title with you. Check with consulates or embassies for the destination country to verify what, if any, additional documents are required for the shipment.

Cars cannot be used as a shipping container. Steamship lines allow automobiles to carry only their own equipment, i.e., a spare tire and tire jack. The doors of your vehicle will not be locked during shipment.

🏠 Understand the type and extent of insurance coverage that your employer will provide.

🏠 Know whether mandatory "in country" insurance will be assessed regardless of previously purchased insurance.

🏠 Purchase insurance in your own country before you move if no insurance requirement exists in your destination country. In the United States, the amount of coverage can be based on the "Blue Book Value" of vehicles.

🏠 Ensure that the insurance you purchase in your own country is effective upon your arrival in the new country.

🏠 Have your car fully serviced before transporting it overseas.

🏠 Know the types of gasoline that will be available.

In this country when you shake hands with a child, you are showing respect to his or her parents.

BANKING NOTES

In this country you should not sit with your legs crossed because it is considered an insult to show the sole of your shoe to another person.

BANK / FINANCE

Delayed overseas mail, unfamiliar foreign banks and closing home country accounts can all contribute to financial headaches — not to mention ruined credit. Take precautions to ensure a smooth transition of your finances when moving abroad and upon returning to your home country. Following are three important financial areas to consider:

- establish a bank account in the foreign country,
- maintain a sound credit record in your own country as well as in the foreign country,
- secure a comprehensive relocation package that details salary, taxes and insurance coverage from your employer.

BEFORE YOU MOVE

Allow six weeks to investigate worldwide financial institutions so personal reference checks and paperwork can be completed. It will simplify your personal financial situation if you select a bank with automated teller machines that can be accessed in both your home country and your destination country. Review and understand your corporate relocation compensation package.

VERIFY THESE FINANCIAL DETAILS

- ☐ income (currency type)
- ☐ amount of personal family trips home and compensation
- ☐ tax equalization details
- ☐ tax return preparation reimbursement
- ☐ trip coverage to home country for unusual circumstances
- ☐ insurance options
- ☐ coverage for medical and household goods
- ☐ housing options and compensation
- ☐ overseas relocation services and assistance
- ☐ working spouse assistance

23

❏ regulations for negotiable securities and the amount of currency that can be taken abroad

❏ tax deductible moving expenses

ESTATE PLANNING

Update your will and estate plan before you move abroad. Your new plan should reflect changes in family, such as a marriage or death or a marital status, personal assets or property purchases. If you purchase property while living overseas, changes will again have to be made in your estate planning. Because the rules vary from state to state and country to country, estate planning, just as insurance planning, should be routinely updated.

IN ADDITION

❏ Have your paycheck automatically deposited into your home country bank or credit union account. You can then arrange automatic payments for mortgages, loans and credit card accounts to ensure on-time payments while you live abroad.

❏ Keep careful records of all accounts and payments of same. Write down account numbers, contact names, addresses and telephone numbers in case of problems.

❏ Discuss investment maintenance with your financial advisor.

❏ Notify your bank, stockbroker and mutual fund company of your new address.

BANKING CHECKLIST

Ask your employer and colleagues to recommend a bank and inquire about their services and reputation.

CONSIDERATIONS

❏ fees for account maintenance

❏ automatic deposit system

❏ hours of operation

❏ internet accessibility (If a bank offers this service, customers are able to write and mail checks electronically.)

❏ overdraft protection

❏ savings programs or special personal services

❏ 24-hour toll-free number

❐ special offers for new clients

❐ affiliations with international services

❐ withdrawal limits for ATMs

❐ free checking, interest checking and safety deposit boxes

Have some currency converted into assorted denominations of paper and coins for your new country in advance so your family can become familiar with the money. Future planning should include purchasing Travelers' Checks in the country's currency as they are accepted by many shops and restaurants. Also take currency for transportation and tipping at your destination. The amount of currency you can carry with you will depend on the limit imposed by a particular country.

See also "Travel Warnings" on page 101 for an Internet site to learn about currency limits.

WHILE ABROAD

The following tips will help you to establish yourself abroad and smoothly transition your finances back home.

▦ Record payments, save receipts and pay accounts in full.

▦ Know the rules for goods purchased overseas, i.e., the cost, date or whether the articles were duty-free or gifts.

▦ Use your home country credit cards once every six months to keep them active.

▦ Review corporate reimbursements after you have lived in the foreign country for six months.

▦ Use credit cards for purchases to get a better exchange rate.

▦ Contact your country's embassy in the foreign countries for income tax assistance.

RE-ESTABLISHING BANKING SERVICES

If you live overseas for more than two to three years, you can smooth your financial transition back to your home country by planning ahead. Request qualifying letters from people such as your bank manager and your employer. These individuals can verify your recent financial and employment status.

⌂ If applying for a major loan or mortgage, write to or visit the bank manager or vice president of a lending institution. Without speaking with the appropriate authority to handle these matters, you may be turned down for credit.

⌂ Take overseas paid-in-full records and recommendation letters with you when applying for (home) credit.

⌂ Explain your unusual circumstances (of being out of the country) to the bank manager.

⌂ When applying for new credit card accounts, seek a small charge limit, and later request an increase.

RELOCATION AND TAX DEDUCTIONS

In the United States, you can call the Internal Revenue Service (IRS) at (800) 829-3676 and request Moving Publication #521 (form #3903) which lists tax deductible moving expenditures. The deductibles include meals, lodging, travel and possibly baby-sitting and kennel fees. There are also other forms you can obtain by calling this 800 number, such as "Selling Your Home" and "Tax Guide" for US citizens living abroad.

Finally, if you are moving as a result of a new job search, know that the expenses incurred may also be tax deductible. A few to consider are postage, telephone calls, interview travel costs, résumé printing costs and employment agency fees.

> *In this country you should not photograph members of the Indian population without first asking permission. (The village mountain people believe taking pictures of children will take their souls away.)*

MEDICAL CARE

Physicians recommend that every person who is moving abroad undergo thorough medical, dental and eye examinations before he or she departs. When visiting your physicians, ask them to prepare copies of your medical records for you to take abroad. Also, compile a complete medical file for all family members. An estimated 25 percent of people who travel or move abroad each year experience a medical problem or a medical emergency. *Don't move abroad unprepared!*

Regarding medications and treatment, know if the same prescriptions/treatments are available in the destination country and what your alternatives are if they are not. Be sure that your family is adequately immunized and know if there are any food or water restrictions in the country to which you are moving.

Another medical consideration is the legality of drugs. Medications that are legal in one country may be illegal in another. If you are taking prescription medications, you should obtain written proof from your doctor that you are supposed to be taking these drugs, as well as the reason for the prescriptions.

The Centers for Disease Control have updated information about specific countries. In the United States you can call (888) 232-3228 or FAX: (888) 232-3299 for information. More details about The Centers for Disease Control are listed on page 101.

A recommended worldwide resource for English- or French-speaking doctors and other medical benefits is THE INTERNATIONAL ASSOCIATION FOR MEDICAL ASSISTANCE TO TRAVELERS (IAMAT). This organization can be contacted in the US at (716) 754-4883, 8 AM to 4 PM ET. (IAMAT is also listed on page 104.)

See also "Medical Checklist" on page 86.

> *In this country it is proper to address surgeons and dentists as "Mister" instead of "Doctor."*

ELDER CARE NOTES

_____

_____

_____

_____

_____

_____

_____

_____

_____

_____

_____

_____

_____

_____

_____

_____

_____

_____

_____

_____

_____

_____

*In this country it is socially unacceptable to have
more wine than you can graciously consume.*

ELDER CARE

Nearly one in three workers in the United States have elder care responsibilities. If you are caring for an aging family member, or believe that you may soon have this responsibility, assuring safe and comfortable care is a primary concern. Realistically evaluate the care that will be required and his or her financial situation. Ask your employer about having an allowance for additional trips home to check on relatives included in your corporate relocation package.

Points to help you evaluate your relative's care are:

▦ whether your relative can drive safely,

▦ the amount of friends from whom he or she can obtain help,

▦ significant physical challenges.

Whether researching a home care provider, an assisted living facility or a nursing home, this checklist has questions you should ask to evaluate appropriate care.

❏ Is the staff or facility licensed and accredited?

❏ Will nurses or therapists evaluate the patient's needs?

❏ Will my family be included in developing a plan of care?

❏ Do you assign supervisors to oversee the quality of care patients are receiving? If so, how often?

❏ Who can our family call with questions or complaints?

❏ How does the agency follow up on and resolve problems?

❏ How does the agency screen their caregivers?

❏ What are the financial terms and procedures?

❏ What procedures are in place for emergencies?

Request references from doctors, patients or family members who are familiar with the provider's quality of service and visit several facilities before selecting one. More elder care considerations are on pages 31 and 32.

In this country you should never congratulate anyone ahead of an important event such as a birthday or wedding because it is considered bad luck.

ELDER CARE
By Joy Loverde

BEFORE YOU MOVE

Despite your hectic relocation schedule, you need to take the time to get organized, create partnerships and identify resources for long-distance caregiving.

GET ORGANIZED: Develop a file for each parent containing notes, medical/medications history, emergency telephone numbers, copies of important documents and pen and paper to take with you. Routinely update it with all correspondence and communication pertaining to your parents. Copy your parents' Social Security cards, driver's licenses, and proof of health insurance to keep in this file as well. Obtain emergency information. Fill in the "Eldercare Emergency Chart" on page 89. Place a copy of the chart in your file and give one to your parents, key family members, and your parents' neighbors.

CREATE PARTNERSHIPS: Make a list people whom you can rely on to delegate responsibilities, such as routine visits and/or telephone calls to your elders in your absence. Be sure these people can be reached 24 hours a day, seven days a week. List their names, addresses and telephone numbers and keep these in your relatives' files.

CREATE ACCESS. Duplicate your parents' home, car and mailbox keys. Keep one set and give another to family members and a trusted neighbor or friend (or your parents' attorney). All helpers should know how to access gate locks, car garage and telephone answering machine messages.

DISCUSS POWER OF ATTORNEY. This legal document will be required in case you need to make decisions regarding your parents' finances and care.

ARRANGE FOR AN INTERDEPENDENT LIFESTYLE. Most elderly people want to remain in their own homes for as long as it is safe to do so. To accomplish this goal, make use of your partnerships and community organizations, i.e., the Phone Alert League, Postal

31

Carrier Alert and Vial of Life Programs. Regular visits from these services will alert you to any physical, mental or financial problems that develop.

HOUSING AND CARE OPTIONS. Be aware of the many housing and care options for elders. Just a few of these are ECHO Housing, retirement communities, assisted-living facilities and life-care retirement communities. Be well-informed before you enter into an agreement with any facility. If you do not have a long-term care strategy, consider that nursing homes sometimes admit patients on a short-term basis.

AFTER THE MOVE

If you have been assisting your elderly relatives, it is only natural that you will feel a certain amount of guilt and, at times helplessness, when you are overseas. These are normal reactions, and it is therefore extremely important that you have trusted caregivers in place to maintain routine check in systems. In addition you can plan extra trips home, at least in the beginning to assure yourself that all the plans you put in place are working to your satisfaction. You can also stay connected by sharing as much as possible about your family life overseas via frequent correspondence, telephone calls and E-mail.

RESPONDING TO AN ELDERCARE EMERGENCY. Surround yourself with the experts. List people on the Eldercare Emergency Chart on page 89 whom you can call in case a problem or emergency occurs. If changes must be made regarding care, include your parent in the decision-making process whenever possible. Suggestions of people to help you decide if it is necessary for you to see your relative in person would be a nurse on call at the hospital, one or several of the doctors and a family member.

See also The Complete Eldercare Planner on page two and Internet sites regarding education, support and legal advice for elders and caregivers on page 104.

> *To indicate you have finished eating in this country, cross your knife and fork (tines down) in the middle of your plate.*

DOING BUSINESS—NOT AS USUAL

OVERSEAS OPPORTUNITIES

Working in a foreign country is an opportunity that can add a valuable dimension to your career; however, international assignments are a major commitment. Overseas positions should not disrupt career plans, but should become developmental positions. To reach this goal, you need to take control of your own situation. Begin by fully understanding the following:

- the position you will assume overseas,
- your title and authority in the new position,
- how you will integrate into the overseas position,
- how you will stay abreast of corporate focus and strategies while abroad,
- how your skills will be utilized upon repatriation.

UNDERSTANDING YOUR ROLE

Take an active part in planning your overseas transition. It is important that you are able to play an integral part in proposals and strategies both at home and abroad in order to gain respect from the foreign managers with whom you will be working.

Before your assignment officially begins, spend time with the corporate manager you are succeeding. This time should preferably be at the work sight but if that is not possible, make a list of your questions and concerns to discuss before assuming the position. Continuity of work efforts and attitudes will positively impact your goals in the foreign country for you and your company.

LEARNING THE LANGUAGE

If a different language is spoken in your destination country, you should have a basic understanding of it before you move. Begin to learn the language in your home country and continue overseas. The effort to learn the local language is highly regarded in most countries and will have a positive effect on business and personal

33

relationships. Try to avoid slang and clichés from your own country and use references that are meaningful, i.e., refer to months and dates instead of seasons when conversing (Spring in one country may be Autumn in another).

CUSTOMS AND MANNERS

When working abroad, your personal and professional lives will be enhanced by keeping an open mind. Try not to pre-judge people and customs, but instead strive to understand and respect the varied conventions of the country. This is not to imply that you should take on characteristics indicative of the people or the country, but that you simply appreciate the culture. The respect you demonstrate to others and your knowledge of procedures will greatly increase your chance of accomplishing business and personal goals overseas.

For instance, in some countries, it is customary to build personal relationships before conducting business while in others, meetings may begin immediately, replacing the social atmosphere altogether.

When working across cultures, be sensitive to how actions and words are being interpreted. Making presentations with translators and body language can be subtly or drastically different and these differences can greatly impact your business success.

See also "Web of Culture" on page 103 and "Windham International" on page 104.

A FEW SUGGESTIONS

- If there appears to be confusion with a language translation, a reverse interpretation may clarify the point.
- Visual aids, i.e., charts, pictures and diagrams, are especially useful in foreign countries.

MAINTAINING CORPORATE VISIBILITY

While working in an expatriate capacity, one of the most effective ways to stay involved with, and make your accomplishments known to, the corporate office is to have a reliable person, or mentor, represent you.

The person you choose as your mentor should preferably be a senior manager who could have an impact on your career direction and who has a schedule that allows him/her to provide the necessary assistance. Your goal is to stay abreast of home office activities and long-range corporate plans. Mentors have to be chosen with care and with specific goals in mind.

MENTOR SELECTION

THIS PERSON SHOULD BE

- ❏ a senior company employee,
- ❏ dependable,
- ❏ in a position to speak effectively and assertively on your behalf — to the appropriate corporate sources,
- ❏ motivated to do the task,
- ❏ worthy of trust,
- ❏ credible,
- ❏ able to understand the corporate strategy and business focus of your company.

MENTORS NEED TO

- ❏ make your accomplishments known to key personnel,
- ❏ watch for career opportunities for you,
- ❏ place news of you in company publications,
- ❏ arrange for your interaction in company projects and events,
- ❏ keep you tuned into changes that take place during the year(s) you are abroad such as corporate developments, products and policies, present and future business strategies and cultural/climate changes within the company.

WHAT YOU SHOULD DO IF THERE IS NO MENTOR

If a mentor program is not in place in your corporation, or you believe that there is no one to effectively fill the role, you can creatively become your own mentor. With careful planning, and by using all available resources such as publications, company functions and existing networking efforts, you can subtly showcase your overseas accomplishments to your corporate office.

BEFORE AND DURING THE ASSIGNMENT, PLAN TO

❏ objectively evaluate the home office climate,

❏ consider the points above,

❏ prioritize your personal efforts,

❏ arrange meetings and/or dine with key personnel while visiting the home office or with these same people when they travel to the foreign office,

❏ obtain a commitment from a company executive for a meaningful assignment and responsibilities upon repatriation,

❏ make any unique challenges known to your corporate advisors which will assist them with future expatriate planning.

In order to fully utilize the valuable knowledge and experience you gain working in another country and culture, you have to understand how you will fit into present and future corporate plans. A mentor affiliation is a strategic part of overseas assignments, and engaging the right person(s) needs to be an ongoing effort. If the selected mentor becomes too busy or the job takes that person elsewhere, you would be wise to have one or several other candidates in mind to fill the role.

In this country last names are placed first. Suggestion: Know which is which on proffered business cards and underline surnames. Also have your business card printed on both sides, with a language on each.

SPOUSE CAREER OPTIONS

Nearly 74 percent of employees moving to a foreign country have a partner with a separate career. If your partner is evaluating an overseas career transfer, you have a major decision to make regarding your own career. For most people, a job means more to them than just a paycheck. In addition to accumulated benefits and prestige, a job is a form of identity. You need to carefully evaluate the situation as it pertains to your family's circumstances, as well as to your own, and your partner's, career opportunities.

When faced with a career disruption, you may consider whether you want to stay in your same career path, redirect your career or pursue a personal interest. Here are four options to consider.

REMAIN AT HOME

Though this may not be your ideal choice, your family situation may require it, or a short-term overseas assignment may make it feasible. This option will mean maintaining a commuter marriage or partnership. Therefore you have to evaluate your family situation and how a foreign relocation could potentially impact everyone. Consider your family's needs, children's ages and everyone's activities and priorities at the point in time of the proposed assignment. If you choose this arrangement, it is important to plan how you will manage frequent reunions and how you will communicate for routine, as well as emergency situations. If you don't have an E-mail account, be sure to set one up and negotiate travel for all family members.

WORK ABROAD FOR YOUR CORPORATION

With imaginative thinking, and help from telecommunication devices (i.e. fax machines, E-mail, modems and computers), you may be able to maintain your current position from abroad. If that is not possible, you might be able to contribute to the company in an altogether different capacity by taking courses to

37

increase your knowledge and skills, performing company research or writing papers or a manual. Investigate the resources available in the country to which you are moving and then present your ideas to your employer. Be open to your employer's suggestions as well.

Seek a New Job

In order to work in another country, you will need to thoroughly understand the country's work requirements and environment. These include Visas and work permits; immigration questions, offices and procedures; everyday living/working conditions; the language of the country and the customs and manners.

Update your portfolio to reflect all the skills and experiences that could be relevant to your international job search and think about how you can use this information to create or further a new career. Ask yourself questions such as: "What are my transferable skills and accomplishments?" "What are my talents and what do I enjoy doing?" "What are some of my successes and how did I achieve them?" Evaluate all of the above as well as your present and future career goals.

See also "Necessary Documents" on page 12 and "Dual Career Resources" on page 101.

Redefine Work

Depending on your career, you may choose to take a sabbatical to study abroad and embellish your portfolio, or perform research that is pertinent to your position. To discover an international university that meets your needs in another country, do some research at local universities before you move. There you will find various resources for people who wish to study abroad. Also, search the Internet by institution name, or by inputting the specific country followed by the term "Universities."

See also "Surfing the Web 101" on page 14.

Another way to redefine your work is to volunteer your time and talent. The knowledge and skills that you acquired from former positions can greatly benefit an overseas organization. Volunteer work will add quality non-salaried experience to current professional accomplishments. In addition, it is a respected endeavor that provides an excellent opportunity to network overseas and associate with people who have expertise in different fields and industries.

Keep in mind that volunteer accomplishments need to be listed on résumés in a manner that validates the experience. Think about ways the experiences, services and contacts translate to business expertise, and how they can ultimately become useful to corporate endeavors.

SUMMING IT ALL UP

If you choose one of the last three options, keep a detailed record of your activities, experiences and accomplishments while living overseas. Include a list of the people with whom you have worked, document important dates and record the names of organizations with which you became affiliated. Skills and international accomplishments can increase your value to a corporation. If you will be job-hunting upon your return, compose an eye-catching résumé embellished with any degrees, experience and achievements you acquired.

> *In this country it is considered very rude to discuss business or distribute business cards at a social occasion.*

39

MY CHILDREN'S ACTIVITIES

_____

_____

_____

_____

_____

_____

MY CHILDREN'S CONCERNS

_____

_____

_____

_____

_____

_____

INTERNET SITES FOR CHILDREN

Virtual World Tours is a wonderful site for children to learn about a new country. This site is described on page 105.

Plus, there are more informative and fun sites in *Let's Move Overseas,* our international activity book for children. For a description of this book see page 45. To order, see page 107.

YOUTH CORNER

A significant aspect of achieving a successful move is creating a sound transition plan for the entire family. Children will probably worry less about a move, and be more excited about the new city, if they are involved in the moving process. There are many things children can do to help you, and in the process, make moving more fun for them.

A FEW ACTIVITIES FOR CHILDREN

- Sort through their belongings for outgrown clothing and toys.
- Plan their new bedrooms.
- Learn about the new country with their parents.
- Help with the relocation travel plans.
- Help parents with some of their lists.
- Make lists of items and games that they will want to take along on the trip to the new country.

EMOTIONAL FACTORS

Don't underestimate the effects relocation can have on children. No matter what their ages, listen carefully to your children's concerns and take time to address each one. No two children are alike. Some will slip into a new environment and culture without so much as a casual glance back at their former lifestyle. Others can be profoundly affected by new surroundings and unfamiliar people. Signs that your children are struggling with the adjustment can include any combination of the following:

- sudden reading difficulties,
- changes in attention span or study habits,
- weight loss or gain,
- altered enthusiasm or energy levels,
- strained relationships with you or their siblings,
- disturbed sleep patterns.

41

A true story involves a student who, in the first twelve weeks of entering an overseas high school, lost over 30 pounds due to worrying about college plans and maintaining a certain grade level. Therefore, it is important that you pay close attention to how your children are adjusting, and address any sudden changes immediately. You should also discuss your concerns with their teachers, and if need be, a guidance counselor. International school teachers frequently encounter new students and they are very capable of helping newcomers adjust.

SCHOOL RESEARCH

Before you begin your evaluation of overseas schools, gather together information about your children's current educational materials, as well as courses of study. If necessary, take some of the materials with you on your international school search.

Careful evaluation of schools and correlation of courses will help students realize successful educational matriculation, as well as help them in their personal adjustments. Teenagers (especially those in high school) need the assurance that their college plans will not be compromised because of a relocation to another country. If your children are approaching college age, begin the college application process six months earlier than is customary due to mail delays, time zone differences and interview availability. The combination of international education, cultural experiences and interaction with students from many countries will broaden children's lives and add another dimension to their college applications.

POINTS TO EVALUATE A NEW SCHOOL

- accreditation rating
- faculty (experience and background)
- space availability
- course selection (remedial to advanced placement)
- language instruction
- standardized test scores, university placements and national enrollments
- academic programs of study

▦ school requirements

▦ up-to-date library

▦ classroom computers

▦ extra-curricular activities, such as theater and creative groups, school publications and sports programs

Periodically visit your children's school(s) to meet with the teachers and also to see for yourself how your children are managing their new environment. Establish a routine for homework and initiate discussions about school. Ask your children questions that require specific answers, such as: "What class do you like best? What are you studying in this class? How do you think this subject relates to today's world issues?"

Educational Resources International, Inc. (ERI), (281) 376-4475, provides assessment and selection of appropriate educational options for students at different age/grade levels.

See also "Education" on page 102 for Internet resources to locate primary and secondary schools, higher educational institutions, educational options and international school guides.

CHILDREN AND SCHOOL SAFETY

Understand the school's safety policy during school hours, and for after-school activities. If you have young children, know if there is a before- and after-school program for their care.

❏ Explain to your children the rules and regulations for playground activities, and ways to deal with strangers.

❏ Have children learn their school bus or train number.

❏ Tell children to wait until the bus comes to a complete stop before entering or exiting.

❏ Tell children to enter and exit cars only at a close/safe area near the school.

See also page 56 for more safety tips for children.

BOARDING SCHOOLS

Depending on the country to which you are moving, boarding schools may be a common educational alternative for your child.

43

The previous guidelines to select quality schools in "School Research" can also help you evaluate boarding schools.
In addition, think about the following:

- daily regimen of the school,
- type of supervision,
- academic schedule,
- study requirements,
- meal schedule and diet,
- type of leisure activities,
- available transportation,
- supervision for on- and off-campus activities,
- amount of free time,
- amount of money your children will need.

During your interview at the boarding school, find out what is expected of your children academically as well as what their daily life will be like. If a boarding school regimen will be a change in lifestyle, it can cause additional stress to that already experienced by living in a new country.

No matter what the ages of your children or their disposition, never assume to know exactly how they will react to a change such as an international relocation. Review the above points and consider additional issues that you believe are relevant to your children and family situation.

ALTERNATIVE TO MOVING
HIGH SCHOOL SENIORS

If you have children who are, or soon will be, seniors in high school you may consider allowing them to stay in their present country with a trusted adult. If you select this option, many details need to be evaluated. Most importantly, recognize that frequent contact and moral support must be continued during your assignment. Don't underestimate the effect that a vast distance and varying time zones can have on you and your family.

Following are just a few points that you and your children need to thoroughly understand:

44

- how, when and where you will see one another;
- the estimated number of trips each of you can make to see one another;
- dialing procedures to call emergency, police, fire and ambulance services;
- their curfew guidelines;
- their financial limitations;
- the procedures for routine and emergency issues, such as medical care and the names and telephone numbers of relevant doctors;
- methods to access funds for routine and emergency needs.

OVERSEAS COLLEGES

Studying abroad can be a unique and maturing experience, educationally and socially. If your college-age children consider this option, research the courses as well as the atmosphere, instructors and schedule of overseas schools. Language needs to be a consideration, even if the college is in an English speaking country. For instance, residents in countries such as New Zealand, England, Canada and Australia all speak English, but with different accents and terminology. Anyone who attends college in another country, needs to understand how the degrees and credits they earn will be valued in their home country. Students who move from country to country need to be sure their hard-earned studies are universally recognized, allowing them to be competitive in other markets.

RESOURCES FOR CHILDREN AND TEENAGERS (See page 107 to order.)

LET'S MOVE OVERSEAS Children can learn about a new country and its language, overseas safety issues and ways to feel at home. Encourages children to express their feelings about moving.

FOOTSTEPS AROUND THE WORLD Helps teens recognize and deal with their complex emotions regarding a move. Also features pouches for tickets and memorabilia, Internet sites and advice from professionals who work with teenagers.

45

NOTES

_____

_____

_____

_____

_____

_____

_____

_____

_____

_____

_____

_____

_____

_____

_____

_____

_____

_____

_____

_____

> *In this country you should never tease someone playfully because it could be misinterpreted and considered offensive.*

PET CARE

Pets can become confused, lost, sick or frightened during a move. On moving days it is best to keep pets in a safe and confined area, on a leash or in a portable kennel because doors will be left ajar as the furniture is transported in or out of the house. If your pet is easily excitable, you might consider boarding it or leaving it with a friend until the move is complete.

TRAVEL NECESSITIES

- ❏ veterinarian papers with medical records
- ❏ pet's bed or article of clothing from a family member
- ❏ leash or harness
- ❏ favorite toy
- ❏ identification tag
- ❏ portable kennel
- ❏ food
- ❏ dish
- ❏ water

TRAVEL PREPARATION

Airplane travel needs to be booked early to arrange convenient and cooler flight times. You should also understand the laws about quarantine and medical restrictions in the foreign country. Helpful sources of information are the airlines, your international moving company and your veterinarian. Ask about transportation, i.e., proper kennel size, food and water restrictions and the required licenses, certificates and vaccinations.

Pets must be at least 10 weeks old for international travel, be in good health and have all of their shots and vaccinations. (You should schedule a thorough health examination and order a new form of identification for your pet before you move.)

YOU NEED TO KNOW THE

- ⊞ costs, which usually include duty and quarantine,
- ⊞ available facilities and veterinarian services,
- ⊞ regulations of the destination country for pets.

See also "Pet/Veterinarian" on page 100.

MOVING COMPANY NOTES

_____

_____

_____

_____

_____

_____

_____

_____

_____

_____

_____

_____

_____

_____

_____

_____

_____

_____

Note: Moving companies commonly provide country specific
information packets. Among the many details they offer are
the climate, time zones, weather, currency and housing and
transportation options in the destination country.

SELECTING A MOVING COMPANY

Survey three well-qualified international firms. Moving companies will send a sales representative to your home to explain the company's services. This person will tour your home to evaluate the packing time and materials required; arrange for pick-up, delivery and storage dates; request the appropriate number of packers and note the estimated weight of your goods. This is the time to ask questions and mention items that require special attention (i.e., antique or fragile furniture). The representative will follow up with a written proposal detailing everything you discussed, including special requests and extra services.

IMPORTANT CONSIDERATIONS

Compare prices, request personal references of satisfied customers and ask these customers questions such as:

- Were the movers on time?
- Were they courteous?
- Did they use runners to protect the floors?
- Were they careful with the furniture?

OTHER SIGNIFICANT POINTS

- costs, services and special discounts
- computerized tracking methods
- on-time pickup and delivery records
- dry, clean and safe storage facilities
- company performance records
- drivers' experience and reliability
- well-maintained trucks and equipment
- appropriate licenses
- costs for packing, mileage and unloading

MOVING INSURANCE

Know how insurance claims will be handled, the amount and type of insurance that is available and ask about additional coverage for your move if necessary. Check the amount against the total value of your personal belongings.

Read the Bill of Lading (a contract describing the goods to be shipped) from the moving company before you sign it. Keep this form in a safe place until your household goods are delivered, charges are paid and any claims are settled.

FOR INSURANCE PURPOSES,

☐ know the rules for boxes packed by owner ("PBO"),

⌂ If you pack a box and it arrives dented and damaged, you can submit a claim for broken goods within that box

⌂ If you pack a box and it arrives without obvious damages or dents, broken items in the box are your responsibility

⌂ Fragile items should be packed by the movers;

☐ understand which materials cannot be moved, i.e., flammable or hazardous materials;

☐ sign all moving company inventory forms after the moving company personnel completes them;

☐ be sure all notations on the inventory form about damaged goods are accurate and signed by you and the company.

INTERNATIONAL GUIDELINES

International moving firms will advise you about regulations and precautions you need to take, such as:

⌂ importations,

⌂ duty declaration,

⌂ foods and personal belongings that can be transported,

⌂ restrictions (which sometimes includes religious items, certain reading material and handguns),

⌂ storage facilities (your goods could be stored for years),

⌂ insurance coverage for stored items and

⌂ overseas services, contact information, telephone number(s) and delivery procedures.

APPLIANCES AND ELECTRONICS

Electrical capabilities vary from country to country. In the United States, appliances are 115 volts, 60 hertz and three wire. In England, they are based on 240 volts, 50 hertz, two wire and single phase. Some countries, such as Japan, even change electrical components from city to city. A knowledgeable international appliance firm can help you determine which appliances can be used in your destination country. Before calling a firm, list your appliances by watts, hertz and volts.

Plug adapters vary by design in almost every country. Adapters change the prongs from one shape to another whereas transformers are required to alter electrical voltage. With the correct adapters and/or transformers, many items can be made to work in other countries. These can be purchased in some electrical stores, but preferably from a specialized international appliance firm.

Home entertainment is another important electronic issue for your family. In addition to electrical variations, each country has a different broadcast system so you might consider purchasing a full multisystem television and video cassette recorder.

See also "Appliance Checklist" on page 82 for space to list your appliances and "Video Overseas" on page 105 for advice on moving appliances from country to country.

MOVE, SELL OR STORE

Some appliances can be used overseas just as they are, some will require a transformer and others should be stored until your return and replaced by another brand. When evaluating what to move, consider the available space in the new home, as well as the cost to operate them. Electricity can be very expensive in some countries and appliance sizes vary as well. Another concern is the cost and availability for parts and services for your appliances. Look into these issues during your pre-move visit to the new country.

THE CONNECTIONS

☐ Color code cords and connectors of items such as computers, stereos, VCRs and televisions for simplified reassembly.

☐ Place correct wires, components and literature in a labeled plastic bag and tape it to or pack within the appliance.

☐ Pack remote controls with the correct electrical appliance or in designated and well-marked boxes.

☐ List serial numbers of computers, appliances and electronics.

Don't overlook safety items such as night lights, electrical timers and flashlights/torches that will work in the destination country. Advance preparation, plus appliance and electrical evaluation will smooth your move and save you time, money, unnecessary hassles and extend the life of your appliances.

In this country you will insult your hosts if you leave a dinner party early. Hint: People here love to visit until the wee hours of the morning.

FACT FINDING TRIP

Research the following details for the new country, preferably on your pre-move visit. Advance preparation will help you to adapt more quickly overseas, and in case an emergency arises (as it often does during a move), you will be prepared.

Most companies allow one or more pre-move visits to the city to which you are moving. Take advantage of this time to locate not only your new home, but also important services and stores. However, since finding lodging is certainly a primary concern, here are a few tips to think about. Consider the room sizes and measure any crucial areas, particularly the laundry, bedrooms, sitting room and kitchen of any house you consider. Carry with you a camera, tape measure, note pad, pencil and a calculator. Your measurements and photos will help you with furniture and appliance decisions before you move.

WHILE VISITING

❏ Visit schools and interview counselors. Take along descriptions of children's books, readers and special programs.

❏ Take pictures of homes, rooms, schools, the city and places of interest to show your family.

❏ Check the availability of parts and services for appliances you are considering using overseas.

❏ Discover the location of services/businesses that are relevant to your family, i.e., hospitals, banks, newsstands, post offices, gas stations, restaurants and supermarkets.

❏ Understand the country's pet quarantine restrictions.

❏ Obtain informational packets, maps and brochures to help you become familiar with the new country.

❏ Locate your home country's embassy.

❏ Find out if there are fellow expats living in the community.

❏ Check out the methods of required transportation.

❏ Look into local Internet providers so you can easily keep in touch with family and friends after the move.

OUR TRAVEL ITINERARY

_____

_____

_____

_____

_____

_____

_____

_____

_____

_____

_____

_____

_____

_____

_____

_____

_____

_____

_____

_____

> _In this country, women need to be especially sensitive about making a glance or gesture that could be interpreted as flirtatious._

TRAVEL PLANS

After a busy week of organizing and packing for your move, the last challenge you will want to experience is a delay in your travel plans. Pre-move planning will ensure a safe and (relatively) relaxing trip. Items to take with you are listed on page 59.

RESERVATIONS

❐ Make hotel/motel reservations two to four weeks in advance.

❐ If you require plane reservations, you must make them at least three to four weeks in advance for the best prices, especially during the busy season (May through September).

❐ Inform a family member/friend of your travel plans, place of lodging and how to contact you.

❐ Arrange airline travel for your pet.

See also "Travel Preparation" on page 47.

AIRPLANE TRAVEL

If you will be taking a considerable amount of valuable items with you when you move, ask about insurance prior to your trip. Estimate the contents of your luggage and ask the airlines what and how you will be compensated if luggage is lost or damaged. If the value of your personal belongings exceeds the airline's maximum coverage, you can purchase additional insurance coverage from your own agent or at the airline check-in counter. Pack jewelry and other valuables in your carry-on bag.

AUTOMOBILE SAFETY

If you are traveling by car to your next country, be aware of the driving laws of each country through which you travel. You should understand requirements for the use of auto lights, speed limits, passing procedures, safety concerns and emergency procedures. Detail your route on an easy-to-read map and review it with another passenger before you depart. Know the numbers to call for road assistance or emergencies.

55

🚗 Lock your valuable items in the trunk.

🚗 Don't overload the car and obstruct your view.

🚗 Wear seat belts, even with air bags.

PACK THESE ITEMS

❑ insurance and registration cards

❑ first aid kit

❑ spare set of car keys

❑ flashlight and a whistle

❑ battery jumper cables

❑ flare for emergencies

❑ spare clothing and blankets

TRAVEL ADVISORY

Travel Warnings & Consular Information Sheets are available for every country of the world with information about unusual immigration practices, health conditions, minor political disturbances, unusual currency and entry regulations, crime and security information and drug penalties.

See also "Travel Warnings" on page 101.

TRAVEL SAFETY FOR CHILDREN

❑ Urge small children to stay close to a parent in an unfamiliar city.

❑ Have a backup contact telephone number to give children in case they cannot reach a family member.

❑ Teach small children their full names.

❑ Teach children to learn and obey all traffic signals.

❑ Teach children safe pedestrian procedures. For example, they should avoid walking between parked cars, look in all directions before crossing a street and cross only at corners.

❑ Place a business card or contact information numbers for both parents inside your child's backpack.

MONEY TIPS FOR TRAVELERS

⊞ Have several ways to access your money, i.e., ATM card, Travelers' Checks and credit cards. Many foreign machines will not accept PIN numbers with more than four digits.

⊞ Place a thick rubber band around your wallet. The friction of the rubber band against your slacks or coat will ensure that you will feel movement if someone tries to pick your pocket.

⊞ Carry your money separately from your identification. If you are robbed, you will not lose both. Also, keep enough money for cab fare in a separate pocket.

⊞ List your Travelers' Check numbers and keep it separate from the actual documents in case of loss.

⊞ Photocopy all your credit cards, identification and travel documents and leave a copy in a safe place.

MONEY TIPS FOR TRAVELERS is printed with permission from *Overseas Digest,* a free monthly Online publication.

See also "Overseas Digest" on page 104.

MORE TRAVEL TIPS

⊞ Don't carry extra credit cards.

⊞ Take important documents, i.e., birth certificates or passports, with you only when necessary.

⊞ Maintain a list of your credit card and account numbers with expiration dates and customer service telephone numbers to have in case your cards are lost or stolen.

⊞ Don't be careless with your credit card receipts. Account numbers can be copied and used by others.

⊞ You can request a credit card report by contacting either Equifax, Experian or Trans Union credit bureaus at (888) 567-8688.

⊞ Consider picking up new checks in person at your bank instead of having them mailed to you.

> *In this country potted plants are never given to someone who is ill. Reason: A rooted plant has the connotation that you may be next in the ground.*

"To Do" List

_____

_____

_____

_____

_____

_____

_____

_____

_____

_____

_____

_____

_____

_____

_____

_____

_____

_____

_____

_____

_____

_____

_____

_____

THE LAST DETAILS

Several more details need to be completed so that you are organized before the packers arrive on your doorstep. You certainly do not want to have important documents such as airline tickets or passports inadvertently packed. This relocation schedule is based on the assumption that your belongings will be delivered four to six weeks after your family's arrival due to shipping transit.

BEFORE YOU LEAVE

❏ Obtain medications and prescriptions for refills for all family members. *See also* "Medical Checklist" on page 86.

❏ Place large signs marked "MOVING," "STORAGE" or "DO NOT PACK" on appropriate household goods. If there are items that you will need immediately at the new home, accumulate these in a box marked "LAST ON."

❏ Put aside items that you want to transport yourself.

❏ Return all library books and any borrowed items.

❏ Pick up or return all loaned or borrowed items.

❏ Pick up clothing at the dry cleaner.

❏ Empty your safety deposit box at the bank.

❏ Set aside a vacuum cleaner and cleaning supplies.

❏ Be sure the post office personnel has your forwarding address and departure date.

❏ Clean and defrost the refrigerator/freezer.

❏ Clean all appliances that remain in the house.

❏ Drain the washing machine.

ITEMS TO TAKE WITH YOU

Packing everything that you need for four to six weeks, plus possibly school and work supplies, may put a strain on your luggage. Ask your corporate relocation officer about allowing a small air shipment in addition to your luggage.

Suggested items to take along
- ☐ telephone number and directions for your hotel
- ☐ moving company name and telephone number in the destination country
- ☐ telephone number for the estate agent
- ☐ jewelry/fur valuations
- ☐ licenses
- ☐ household inventory
- ☐ moving company inventory
- ☐ keys for new home
- ☐ inoculation records
- ☐ school records
- ☐ list of recommended doctors
- ☐ prescriptions for medications
- ☐ physician and dental records
- ☐ passports, overseas documents and airline tickets
- ☐ children's activities/games and books
- ☐ proof of medical, auto and household goods insurance

DEPARTURE DAY ESSENTIALS
Items commonly needed on moving days are listed so you can purchase and store them in one convenient location. Excess nonperishables can be packed in boxes and marked "LAST ON."

Food and related items
- ☐ food and beverages for moving day
- ☐ paper cups and bags with zipper closures
- ☐ paper plates/napkins/disposable utensils
- ☐ instant coffee/tea/milk/sugar

Essentials
- ☐ aspirin/adhesive bandages
- ☐ first-aid kit
- ☐ paper towels/facial tissue/toilet tissue
- ☐ soap/disposable towelettes

☐ car emergency equipment (if you are driving)
☐ travel alarm
☐ flashlight
☐ small tool kit
☐ large trash bags

"THE KITCHEN DRAWER"

☐ scissors/pocketknife
☐ tape measure/collapsible ruler
☐ can opener/bottle opener/corkscrew
☐ paper/scratch pad/envelopes
☐ pen/pencil/marking pens
☐ cellophane tape/heavy-duty tape

DEPARTURE DAY

☐ Clean and vacuum the house.
☐ Set the house temperature appropriately for the time of year.
☐ Turn off lights, appliances and ovens.
☐ Close and lock windows and doors.
☐ Leave a forwarding address and telephone number with a neighbor.
☐ Check closets, shelves, drawers to permanent cabinets, storage areas, the basement and the garage to be sure that everything has been packed.
☐ Lock your house.
☐ Leave the garage door opener for the next owner.
☐ Give details such as telephone and fax numbers for your destination lodging to your moving company personnel so they can contact you upon arrival in the new location.

In this country you should never give someone a slap on the back because it could be considered rude.

THINGS TO SEE AND PLACES TO GO

_____

_____

_____

_____

_____

_____

_____

_____

_____

_____

_____

_____

_____

_____

_____

_____

_____

_____

_____

_____

_____

In this country staying in a fine hotel creates a better image.

THE NEW CITY

Your family will more than likely be living in temporary quarters for several weeks until your household goods are delivered due to the shipment timing. Use this time to establish services, locate stores and activities, and find basic necessities your family will need. Locating products and services you are accustomed to using can be time consuming in another country. Products may be sold under another name, stores to purchase the products can be very different, or the products may not even exist and you will have to locate a substitute.

LEARNING THE AREA

Brochures, books and train/bus schedules for the new city and country can be found at hotels and motels, relocation services, the visitors' center and real estate agencies. Relocation services also have packages for newcomers that contain a wealth of information about the city. Take your children along on city excursions to help them become acclimated as well. Collect business cards everywhere you go so you can remember the services and store locations. You can also note office hours and convenient directions to the facilities on the back of the card.

THINK ABOUT

- visiting local historical museums and parks,
- taking a walking tour or bus tour of the city,
- dining at restaurants with local cuisine,
- familiarizing your family with the transportation services,
- finding expatriate groups (ask neighbors and co-workers).

NEW HEALTH SERVICES

It was suggested that you research new medical care prior to departing. Accidents and illness often occur during a move; therefore, locate medical facilities, pharmacies and physicians that will meet your family's needs *as soon as possible.* Also understand all procedures for routine and emergency medical care.

See also "New Health Services" on page 87 and "New Medical Care" on page 88.

MOVING IN

Every good move is a cooperative effort between the mover and the family. You or a responsible party should be at your new residence when the movers are scheduled to arrive. Work with your movers and learn their names, using them often.

- Mark your room doors with names, numbers or colors and then refer to them by the designation.
- Take the time to show all the movers the entire home, and acquaint them with each room and your furniture plans.
- Create a furniture floor plan for each room and place the plans inside the rooms. Then tell the movers (instead of dashing around to show them) where to place each piece of furniture as it is brought through the door.
- Have someone available to check the contents of the boxes and take note of dents, damages or missing items.
- Keep pets on a leash or in a portable kennel because doors will be left ajar as the furniture is transported into the house.
- Ask the movers to reassemble items taken apart at origin.

CLAIM PROCEDURE

On moving day check off each item on the inventory sheet as it is delivered. If any of the boxes that were packed by the moving company appear damaged, open them and inspect the contents in the presence of one of the movers. Ask your mover to sign and note the damage on the correct form.

YOU SHOULD KNOW

- how to file an insurance claim if damages occur,
- the time limit to submit a claim,
- the currency used as compensation for damaged goods.

See also "Relocation Insurance" on page 19.

In this country direct eye contact is impolite.

FAMILY TRADITIONS

Family and cultural traditions and celebrations are part and parcel of who we are. Holidays should certainly be remembered and observed at the appropriate times in people's lives no matter where they are living. Celebrating these festivities will ease loneliness and help children preserve continuity in their lives. In addition, these efforts will embellish family life and help families to maintain strong personal bonds.

Relocating to a new country can ultimately become an enriching experience for the entire family. Listed below are suggestions that have worked for many other relocating families. They should speed your own transition and help you and your family settle in and become comfortable in your new community.

Learn something new about your community or country every week.

Hold weekly family meetings to discuss problems anyone is experiencing and to share positive episodes that have occurred to each family member in the past week.

Reach out to make new friends.

Share family stories and old holiday photos with each other and friends.

Share your special celebrations with people from other countries.

Send holiday cards to friends and family in your home country.

Take one day at a time.

ABOUT YOUR MOVE HOME

_____

_____

_____

_____

_____

_____

_____

_____

_____

_____

_____

_____

_____

_____

_____

_____

_____

_____

_____

_____

_____

*In this country people take offense
to foreigners crossing their arms.*

REPATRIATION

Relocation efforts usually focus on the initial move overseas and managing life abroad. The often overlooked issue is moving back *home*. Expatriates generally don't pay much attention to this aspect because they believe they will be returning to a comfortable lifestyle and a familiar environment, but are later shocked to learn that home no longer feels that way.

In some countries you will find organizations that plan transition seminars for families who are moving home. If these are available where you are living, be sure to take advantage of the opportunity. Repatriation, the final adjustment in the overseas relocation process, can be eased by recognizing and planning for the challenges. Successfully repatriating is a process that begins while still living in the foreign country.

BEFORE MOVING HOME

Consider the personality traits, skills and attitudes that you believe were useful to you in adjusting to the foreign culture. These will again prove valuable during repatriation.

IN ADDITION

- Learn about the recent trends in your home country (attire, television shows, sayings, foods and movies).
- Involve your family in open communication about their hopes, fears and expectations about moving home.
- Stress the positive aspects about returning to your home country, such as enjoying former activities and having more contact with relatives.
- Find out as much as possible about the city, the people and the culture to which you are moving.
- If you are returning to your former city, don't assume this will make adaptation easier because changes will have taken place in your absence.

ARRIVING HOME

Plan to rebuild friendships. Former friends may feel ill at ease talking to their now worldly friend who has lived and traveled in other countries.

- Network with other families who have lived overseas. These people can offer you tips about what worked for them, which may also help you readjust to life at home. They may also be able to recommend doctors, schools, child-care facilities and other services.

- Share information about your international experience/ location to your company, schools and community groups.

- Take time with your transition; the adjustment of returning to one's home country is as challenging, if not more so, than moving to a foreign country.

- Consider engaging a repatriation counselor who can assist you in expressing your feelings about the change and work through the challenges that you experience.

- Think about ways you can incorporate your overseas experiences into your home country job efforts.

- Listen and be patient.

- Value colleagues' opinions and efforts.

- Encourage children to retain friendships with the friends they met abroad.

DON'T ...

- Plunge in and make quick changes.

- Compare the overseas office to the home office.

- Continually talk about the wonderful overseas personnel.

- Criticize your colleagues.

- Dominate conversational topics; instead, conscientiously intersperse references to life overseas with activities and interests that have a commonality with your friends at home.

MAKING THE MOST OF YOUR EXPERIENCE

Reentry to one's home country after living in another requires forethought and planning, both personally and professionally.

By taking a few precautions, you can realize a positive and productive transition into your former home. Adults and children alike need to remind themselves of what they have gained from the overseas experience and how they can put that knowledge and experience to use in the best possible way in their home country.

People who travel and live overseas usually become more flexible, knowledgeable, adaptable and versatile. These experiences provide new perspectives and will surely benefit you for the rest of your life. Repatriation shock and feelings of being out of step with a once familiar home environment eventually pass. Upon moving back to your home country, it is important for you to get involved, join a club, volunteer your services and put your experiences to use in a positive manner.

I wish you all the very best!

HOME AWAY FROM HOME

REFERENCE SECTION

This section will help you quickly organize relocation chores.

UTILITY SERVICES TO CANCEL

You will want to have electricity, telephone and heat until the last day of packing. Contact your service providers in advance in case they require several weeks to schedule appointments.

Contacted		Date
☐	cable television	_____
☐	city tax collector	_____
☐	electric	_____
☐	local telephone company	_____
☐	long-distance telephone company	_____
☐	gas	_____
☐	newspaper	_____
☐	oil	_____
☐	postal service	_____
☐	recycling company	_____
☐	refuse company	_____
☐	water	_____
☐	other	
☐	_____	
☐	_____	_____
☐	_____	_____
☐	_____	_____
☐	_____	_____
☐	_____	_____
☐	_____	_____
☐	_____	_____
	_____	_____

See also page 97 for a list to establish new services.

ADDRESS NOTIFICATION

Obtain new cards and/or notify relevant companies and organizations. Each time an invoice or publication comes through your mail slot, add it to the list! Then keep this list for your next move.

Contacted   **Date**

☐   airline frequent flyer cards   _____

☐   bank   _____

☐   car registration   _____

☐   college bursar's offices   _____

☐   company publication   _____

☐   credit cards (see Credit Accounts page 80)   _____

☐   department stores   _____

☐   driver's license   _____

☐   finance/mortgage   _____

☐   insurance companies   _____

☐   Internal Revenue Service   _____

☐   investments   _____

☐   local personal accounts   _____

☐   magazines (see Subscriptions page 81)   _____

☐   social security office   _____

☐   stocks/mutual funds   _____

☐   voter registration   _____

      other

☐   _____   _____

☐   _____   _____

☐   _____   _____

☐   _____   _____

See also pages 74-75 for spaces to list addresses.

73

ADDRESSES TO REMEMBER

Name / address _____

_____

_____

Tel _____ E-mail _____

Name / address _____

_____

_____

Tel _____ E-mail _____

Name / address _____

_____

_____

Tel _____ E-mail _____

Name / address _____

_____

_____

Tel _____ E-mail _____

Name / address _____

_____

_____

Tel _____ E-mail _____

Name / address _____

_____

_____

Tel _____ E-mail _____

Name / address _____

_____

_____

Tel _____ E-mail _____

ADDRESSES TO REMEMBER

Name / address _____
_____
_____
Tel _____ E-mail _____

Name / address _____
_____
_____
Tel _____ E-mail _____

Name / address _____
_____
_____
Tel _____ E-mail _____

Name / address _____
_____
_____
Tel _____ E-mail _____

Name / address _____
_____
_____
Tel _____ E-mail _____

Name / address _____
_____
_____
Tel _____ E-mail _____

Name / address _____
_____
_____
Tel _____ E-mail _____

OFFICIAL PAPERS

This is a good time to review your important family records to update and renew them as necessary. If you have not already done so, guardianship for your children is something you may want to consider as well.

Item   **Location**

Family Records

    Birth certificates   _____

    Guardianship   _____

    Licenses   _____

    Marriage Certificate   _____

    Medical files   _____

    Passports   _____

    Power of Attorney   _____

Finances

    Stocks   _____

    Tax returns   _____

    Wills/estate planning   _____

Insurance

    Health   _____

    Household   _____

    Life   _____

Personal Property

    Auto titles   _____

    Deed to home   _____

    Jewelry/fur valuations   _____

    Household goods
        video/inventory   _____

    Safety deposit box   _____

PERSONAL INVENTORY

On page 19, I suggested ways to document your household goods. The next few pages are provided so you can list your personal belongings by name, date of purchase and valuation.

Article	Date	Value

Continued on next two pages

PERSONAL INVENTORY

Article	Date	Value

PERSONAL INVENTORY

Article	Date	Value

CREDIT ACCOUNTS

Bank _____
Account number _____
Contact _____
Tel _____ Date notified _____

Bank _____
Account number _____
Contact _____
Tel _____ Date notified _____

Financial advisor _____
Account number _____
Contact _____
Tel _____ Date notified _____

Financial advisor _____
Account number _____
Contact _____
Tel _____ Date notified _____

Department store _____
Account number _____
Contact _____
Tel _____ Date notified _____

Department store _____
Account number _____
Contact _____
Tel _____ Date notified _____

Department store _____
Account number _____
Contact _____
Tel _____ Date notified _____

FAMILY TRADITIONS

Family and cultural traditions and celebrations are part and parcel of who we are. Holidays should certainly be remembered and observed at the appropriate times in people's lives no matter where they are living. Celebrating these festivities will ease loneliness and help children preserve continuity in their lives. In addition, these efforts will embellish family life and help families to maintain strong personal bonds.

Relocating to a new country can ultimately become an enriching experience for the entire family. Listed below are suggestions that have worked for many other relocating families. They should speed your own transition and help you and your family settle in and become comfortable in your new community.

Learn something new about your community or country every week.

Hold weekly family meetings to discuss problems anyone is experiencing and to share positive episodes that have occurred to each family member in the past week.

Reach out to make new friends.

Share family stories and old holiday photos with each other and friends.

Share your special celebrations with people from other countries.

Send holiday cards to friends and family in your home country.

Take one day at a time.

ABOUT YOUR MOVE HOME

_____

_____

_____

_____

_____

_____

_____

_____

_____

_____

_____

_____

_____

_____

_____

_____

_____

_____

_____

_____

_____

*In this country people take offense
to foreigners crossing their arms.*

REPATRIATION

Relocation efforts usually focus on the initial move overseas and managing life abroad. The often overlooked issue is moving back *home*. Expatriates generally don't pay much attention to this aspect because they believe they will be returning to a comfortable lifestyle and a familiar environment, but are later shocked to learn that home no longer feels that way.

In some countries you will find organizations that plan transition seminars for families who are moving home. If these are available where you are living, be sure to take advantage of the opportunity. Repatriation, the final adjustment in the overseas relocation process, can be eased by recognizing and planning for the challenges. Successfully repatriating is a process that begins while still living in the foreign country.

BEFORE MOVING HOME

Consider the personality traits, skills and attitudes that you believe were useful to you in adjusting to the foreign culture. These will again prove valuable during repatriation.

IN ADDITION

- Learn about the recent trends in your home country (attire, television shows, sayings, foods and movies).
- Involve your family in open communication about their hopes, fears and expectations about moving home.
- Stress the positive aspects about returning to your home country, such as enjoying former activities and having more contact with relatives.
- Find out as much as possible about the city, the people and the culture to which you are moving.
- If you are returning to your former city, don't assume this will make adaptation easier because changes will have taken place in your absence.

67

ARRIVING HOME

Plan to rebuild friendships. Former friends may feel ill at ease talking to their now worldly friend who has lived and traveled in other countries.

- Network with other families who have lived overseas. These people can offer you tips about what worked for them, which may also help you readjust to life at home. They may also be able to recommend doctors, schools, child-care facilities and other services.
- Share information about your international experience/location to your company, schools and community groups.
- Take time with your transition; the adjustment of returning to one's home country is as challenging, if not more so, than moving to a foreign country.
- Consider engaging a repatriation counselor who can assist you in expressing your feelings about the change and work through the challenges that you experience.
- Think about ways you can incorporate your overseas experiences into your home country job efforts.
- Listen and be patient.
- Value colleagues' opinions and efforts.
- Encourage children to retain friendships with the friends they met abroad.

DON'T ...

- Plunge in and make quick changes.
- Compare the overseas office to the home office.
- Continually talk about the wonderful overseas personnel.
- Criticize your colleagues.
- Dominate conversational topics; instead, conscientiously intersperse references to life overseas with activities and interests that have a commonality with your friends at home.

MAKING THE MOST OF YOUR EXPERIENCE

Reentry to one's home country after living in another requires forethought and planning, both personally and professionally.

By taking a few precautions, you can realize a positive and productive transition into your former home. Adults and children alike need to remind themselves of what they have gained from the overseas experience and how they can put that knowledge and experience to use in the best possible way in their home country.

People who travel and live overseas usually become more flexible, knowledgeable, adaptable and versatile. These experiences provide new perspectives and will surely benefit you for the rest of your life. Repatriation shock and feelings of being out of step with a once familiar home environment eventually pass. Upon moving back to your home country, it is important for you to get involved, join a club, volunteer your services and put your experiences to use in a positive manner.

I wish you all the very best!

REFERENCE SECTION

This section will help you quickly organize relocation chores.

UTILITY SERVICES TO CANCEL

You will want to have electricity, telephone and heat until the last day of packing. Contact your service providers in advance in case they require several weeks to schedule appointments.

Contacted   **Date**

☐   cable television   _____

☐   city tax collector   _____

☐   electric   _____

☐   local telephone company   _____

☐   long-distance telephone company   _____

☐   gas   _____

☐   newspaper   _____

☐   oil   _____

☐   postal service   _____

☐   recycling company   _____

☐   refuse company   _____

☐   water   _____

☐   other   _____

☐   _____   _____

☐   _____   _____

☐   _____   _____

☐   _____   _____

☐   _____   _____

☐   _____   _____

☐   _____   _____

See also page 97 for a list to establish new services.

ADDRESS NOTIFICATION

Obtain new cards and/or notify relevant companies and organizations. Each time an invoice or publication comes through your mail slot, add it to the list! Then keep this list for your next move.

Contacted   **Date**

☐   airline frequent flyer cards   _____

☐   bank   _____

☐   car registration   _____

☐   college bursar's offices   _____

☐   company publication   _____

☐   credit cards (see Credit Accounts page 80)   _____

☐   department stores   _____

☐   driver's license   _____

☐   finance/mortgage   _____

☐   insurance companies   _____

☐   Internal Revenue Service   _____

☐   investments   _____

☐   local personal accounts   _____

☐   magazines (see Subscriptions page 81)   _____

☐   social security office   _____

☐   stocks/mutual funds   _____

☐   voter registration   _____

     other

☐   _____   _____

☐   _____   _____

☐   _____   _____

☐   _____   _____

See also pages 74-75 for spaces to list addresses.

ADDRESSES TO REMEMBER

Name / address _____

_____

_____

Tel _____ E-mail _____

Name / address _____

_____

_____

Tel _____ E-mail _____

Name / address _____

_____

_____

Tel _____ E-mail _____

Name / address _____

_____

_____

Tel _____ E-mail _____

Name / address _____

_____

_____

Tel _____ E-mail _____

Name / address _____

_____

_____

Tel _____ E-mail _____

Name / address _____

_____

_____

Tel _____ E-mail _____

ADDRESSES TO REMEMBER

Name / address _____
_____
_____

Tel _____ E-mail _____

Name / address _____
_____
_____

Tel _____ E-mail _____

Name / address _____
_____
_____

Tel _____ E-mail _____

Name / address _____
_____
_____

Tel _____ E-mail _____

Name / address _____
_____
_____

Tel _____ E-mail _____

Name / address _____
_____
_____

Tel _____ E-mail _____

Name / address _____
_____
_____

Tel _____ E-mail _____

OFFICIAL PAPERS

This is a good time to review your important family records to update and renew them as necessary. If you have not already done so, guardianship for your children is something you may want to consider as well.

Item	Location
Family Records	
Birth certificates	_____
Guardianship	_____
Licenses	_____
Marriage Certificate	_____
Medical files	_____
Passports	_____
Power of Attorney	_____
Finances	
Stocks	_____
Tax returns	_____
Wills/estate planning	_____
Insurance	
Health	_____
Household	_____
Life	_____
Personal Property	
Auto titles	_____
Deed to home	_____
Jewelry/fur valuations	_____
Household goods video/inventory	_____
Safety deposit box	_____

PERSONAL INVENTORY

On page 19, I suggested ways to document your household goods. The next few pages are provided so you can list your personal belongings by name, date of purchase and valuation.

Article	Date	Value

Continued on next two pages

PERSONAL INVENTORY

Article	Date	Value

Personal Inventory

Article	Date	Value

CREDIT ACCOUNTS

Bank _____
Account number _____
Contact _____
Tel _____ Date notified _____

Bank _____
Account number _____
Contact _____
Tel _____ Date notified _____

Financial advisor _____
Account number _____
Contact _____
Tel _____ Date notified _____

Financial advisor _____
Account number _____
Contact _____
Tel _____ Date notified _____

Department store _____
Account number _____
Contact _____
Tel _____ Date notified _____

Department store _____
Account number _____
Contact _____
Tel _____ Date notified _____

Department store _____
Account number _____
Contact _____
Tel _____ Date notified _____

FAMILY SUBSCRIPTIONS

Publication _____
Notification date _____

Publication _____
Notification date _____

Publication _____
Notification date _____

Publication _____
Notification date _____

Publication _____
Notification date _____

Publication _____
Notification date _____

Publication _____
Notification date _____

Publication _____
Notification date _____

Publication _____
Notification date _____

Publication _____
Notification date _____

Publication _____
Notification date _____

Publication _____
Notification date _____

Publication _____
Notification date _____

APPLIANCE CHECKLIST

List the watts, hertz and volts of the appliances you want to move.
Check the last column for any models that need to be replaced.

Appliance	Watts/Hertz/Volts/Amp.	Replace
clothes washer	_____	_____
clothes dryer	_____	_____
refrigerator	_____	_____
microwave	_____	_____
lamps	_____	_____
telephones	_____	_____
answering machine	_____	_____
facsimile	_____	_____
radio/stereo	_____	_____
coffee machine	_____	_____
espresso machine	_____	_____
blender/mixer	_____	_____
food processor	_____	_____
television	_____	_____
video recorder	_____	_____
computer	_____	_____
printer	_____	_____
exercise machine	_____	_____
humidifier	_____	_____
other	_____	_____
	_____	_____
	_____	_____
	_____	_____

INSURANCE

Carrier_____
Policy no._____ Plan _____
Contact _____
Tel _____Claims_____
Date notified _____
Address _____

Carrier_____
Policy no._____ Plan _____
Contact _____
Tel _____Claims_____
Date notified _____
Address _____

Carrier_____
Policy no._____ Plan _____
Contact _____
Tel _____Claims_____
Date notified _____
Address _____

Carrier_____
Policy no._____ Plan _____
Contact _____
Tel _____Claims_____
Date notified _____
Address _____

CURRENT PHYSICIANS AND CONTACTS

Physician _____

Family member_____

Tel _____ Contact _____

Address _____

_____

Condition _____

Follow up _____

Physician _____

Family member_____

Tel _____ Contact _____

Address _____

_____

Condition _____

Follow up _____

Physician _____

Family member_____

Tel _____ Contact _____

Address _____

_____

Condition _____

Follow up _____

Physician _____

Family member_____

Tel _____ Contact _____

Address _____

_____

Condition _____

Follow up _____

CURRENT PHYSICIANS AND CONTACTS

Physician _____
Family member_____
Tel _____ Contact _____
Address _____

Condition _____
Follow up _____

Physician _____
Family member_____
Tel _____ Contact _____
Address _____

Condition _____
Follow up _____

Physician _____
Family member_____
Tel _____ Contact _____
Address _____

Condition _____
Follow up _____

Physician _____
Family member_____
Tel _____ Contact _____
Address _____

Condition _____
Follow up _____

MEDICAL CHECKLIST

This checklist will complement the medical recommendations that were described on page 27.

☐ Pack your family's medical records that document illnesses, surgery, broken bones and emergency ward visits.

☐ Take with you the addresses and telephone numbers of your home country doctors, dentists and pharmacist.

☐ Take enough prescription medications for at least six months, plus refill prescriptions.

☐ Keep all medications in their own labeled containers, noting the strength, dosage and name of physicians.

☐ Know the side effects of everyone's medications.

☐ Know the generic name of each medication so that you can obtain them, or similar products, overseas.

☐ Ask your current doctors how to obtain doctors and/or specialists who speak your language in the new country.

☐ Pack a bilingual dictionary.

☐ Pack an anti-diarrhea medicine and an antibiotic if you are prone to severe infections when traveling abroad.

☐ Take along your eye care prescriptions, as well as extra supplies.

☐ Understand the procedure, telephone numbers and access codes to locate emergency care, i.e., the equivalent of 911.

☐ Know your alternatives if your medical plan will not be valid in the foreign country.

☐ Carry with you insurance forms and a medical identification card.

Note: Discover the Poison Control Center in your new location and the procedures to obtain help in case of an emergency.

others

☐ _____

☐ _____

HOME AWAY FROM HOME

NEW HEALTH SERVICES

Physician-patient compatibility is as important as the quality of service you receive, especially in a different culture. Take the time to meet with doctors you are considering before an accident or illness occurs within your family.

For new physician services, consider:
- ❐ fluency of language
- ❐ references from reliable sources
- ❐ accessibility of the office
- ❐ diversity of care
- ❐ accepted insurance
- ❐ terms, conditions and method of payment if insurance is not accepted
- ❐ qualifications of the physicians
- ❐ physicians referral network
- ❐ hours of availability
- ❐ back-up care in case of an emergency
- ❐ hospitals with which the physicians are affiliated
- ❐ services provided by the hospitals (for instance, not all hospitals have emergency or casualty services)

others
- ❐ _____
- ❐ _____
- ❐ _____
- ❐ _____

See also "IAMAT" on page 104 to locate English- or French-speaking doctors.

> *In this country never use your left hand to accept a gift.*

HOME AWAY FROM HOME

NEW MEDICAL CARE

Physician _____
Family member _____
Tel _____ Contact _____
Address _____
_____
Condition _____
Follow up _____

Physician _____
Family member _____
Tel _____ Contact _____
Address _____
_____
Condition _____
Follow up _____

Physician _____
Family member _____
Tel _____ Contact _____
Address _____
_____
Condition _____
Follow up _____

Physician _____
Family member _____
Tel _____ Contact _____
Address _____
_____
Condition _____
Follow up _____

ELDERCARE EMERGENCY CHART

Full name _____

Address _____

_____

Telephone _____

Date of birth _____

Social Security number _____

Medicare health insurance/policy number_____

Allergies _____

Blood type _____

Current medications (name and purpose) _____

_____

Learn the 911 equivalent for ambulance, fire and police emergencies.

Health Care		**Network**	
Doctor	_____	Family	_____
Doctor	_____	Family	_____
Dentist	_____	Family	_____
Hospital	_____	Neighbor	_____
24 hr. pharmacy	_____	Neighbor	_____
Aging agency	_____	Friend	_____
Nursing agency	_____	Friend	_____
Health insurance	_____	Senior center	_____
_____		Social worker	_____
_____		Clergy	_____
_____		Church group	_____
_____		Co-worker	_____

Services			
Electrician	_____	Landlord	_____
Electric Co.	_____	Banker	_____
Water Co.	_____	Attorney	_____
Gas Co.	_____	Accountant	_____
TV cable	_____	Insurance agent	_____
Plumber	_____	House alarm	_____
Home care	_____	Locksmith	_____
House sitter	_____	Pet sitter	_____

© Copyright *The Complete Eldercare Planner.* Reprinted with permission.

SCHOOL REQUIREMENTS

Child's name _____

Current school _____

Years in attendance _____

Address _____

_____

Contact _____ Tel _____

School records   **Comments**

☐ Achievement tests _____

☐ Medical history   _____

☐ Transcripts   _____

☐ Other   _____

Academic level _____

Text books   _____ _____

                     _____ _____

                     _____ _____

New school _____

Address _____

_____

Contact _____ Tel _____

Paperwork received   **Comments**

☐ Achievement tests _____

☐ Medical history   _____

☐ Transcripts   _____

☐ Other   _____

☐   _____

SCHOOL REQUIREMENTS

Child's name _____

Current school _____

Years in attendance _____

Address _____

_____

Contact _____ Tel _____

School records   **Comments**

❏ Achievement tests _____

❏ Medical history _____

❏ Transcripts _____

❏ Other _____

Academic level _____

Text books _____

_____

_____

New school _____

Address _____

_____

Contact _____ Tel _____

Paperwork received   **Comments**

❏ Achievement tests _____

❏ Medical history _____

❏ Transcripts _____

❏ Other _____

❏ _____

HOUSE HUNTING NOTES

_____

_____

_____

_____

_____

_____

_____

_____

_____

_____

_____

_____

_____

_____

_____

_____

_____

_____

_____

_____

_____

_____

_____

MOVING COMPANY

Origination company _____

Agent _____

Address _____

_____

Tel _____ Fax _____

Moving dates _____

Destination company _____

Contact _____

Anticipated arrival of goods _____

Special details _____

_____

_____

_____

_____

_____

REAL ESTATE

Origination company _____

Agent _____

Address _____

_____

Tel _____ Fax _____

Overseas contact _____

_____

Destination company _____

Agent _____

Address _____

_____

Tel _____ Fax _____

_____

93

LODGING / TRAVEL

Hotel _____

Tel _____ Fax _____

E-mail address _____

Date of arrival _____

Date of departure _____

Address _____

_____

_____

Directions/other information _____

_____

_____

_____

TRAVELERS' CHECKS

Banking source _____

Check nos. from _____ to _____

Currency _____

Denomination _____

Number to call for questions or loss _____

Checks in the name of _____

Banking source _____

Checks from _____ to _____

Currency _____

Denomination _____

Number to call for questions or loss _____

Checks in the name of _____

Note: Keep records of all travel expenses with amounts, dates and relevant information regarding the expense. A pouch is provided in the back of the book for these receipts. If you are moving as a result of a job change, note the deductibles mentioned on page 26 that can be claimed on your income tax.

SETTLING IN CHECKLIST

Take advantage of relocation services (see "Relocation" in the new country's telephone directory) for help to learn about the new city and country. You will also want to

☐ subscribe to a newspaper;

☐ confirm that all insurance policies are in place and check on new auto insurance coverage within 30 days of arriving;

☐ have your children visit the school before their first day;

☐ arrange for your children to meet some new children such as classmates and/or neighborhood residents;

☐ check with the post office personnel to be sure they have your new address;

☐ find out what you will need to do to obtain a new driver's license, such as learn local driving laws and driving regulations, study a new manual and take a test;

☐ research organizations, schools and continuing education;

☐ check out shopping areas and places of interest;

☐ try out your new Internet service to assure you can keep in touch with former friends and family members.

CHILDHOOD SAFETY

Be sure that your children understand the safety issues in and around your community, as well as the new school's rules and regulations. In addition, it's a good idea to create a file for your children which includes details such as their social security numbers, weight, height, nicknames and other distinguishing features. Plan to update this file on a regular basis with photos and personal details.

A FEW MORE TIPS

☐ Get involved in school and community activities.

☐ Purchase a country-specific cookbook to simplify meal preparation and to avoid the necessity of converting measurements and oven temperatures.

- ❐ Call a friend in your home country on weekends when the rates are low.
- ❐ Learn about your new culture and the language.
- ❐ Try new foods and go on tours.
- ❐ Send a scenic postcard to friends and relatives.
- ❐ Take advantage of every possible moment and find positive elements about the new country.
- ❐ Learn where you can purchase home country newspapers and/or arrange to have newspapers mailed to you.

NEW UTILITY SERVICES

Your estate agent or landlord can help you locate new utility and household services. Establish these services before you move in, especially the electricity, telephone and heat.

Notified   **Date**

☐   cable television   _____
☐   city tax collector   _____
☐   electric   _____
☐   local telephone company   _____
☐   long-distance telephone company   _____
☐   gas   _____
☐   newspaper   _____
☐   oil   _____
☐   postal service   _____
☐   recycling company   _____
☐   refuse company   _____
☐   water   _____

     other

☐   _____   _____
☐   _____   _____
☐   _____   _____
☐   _____   _____
☐   _____   _____
☐   _____   _____
☐   _____   _____
☐   _____   _____
☐   _____   _____

In this country, crossing your fingers is considered offensive.

NEW LOCATION

Locate as soon as possible

☐ the nearest hospital _____

☐ fire/police departments _____

_____

☐ pharmacy _____

☐ place of worship _____

☐ convenient bank branch _____

☐ beauty/barber shops _____

_____

☐ transportation service _____

☐ school and bus stop _____

_____

☐ doctors' and dentists' offices (see "New Medical Care" on page 88)

☐ veterinary office/pet hospital _____

_____

☐ pet food/supplies _____

☐ plumber/repair services _____

_____

☐ dry cleaner _____

☐ shopping centers _____

_____

☐ market _____

☐ restaurants _____

_____

other _____

_____

SAFETY CHECKLIST

Use well-traveled routes in new cities. Be sure your family knows the telephone numbers and street addresses for home and work.

TRAVEL TIPS

- ☐ Before leaving home, inform a family member of your travel plans, route of travel and how to contact you.
- ☐ Always carry a passport or an identification card.
- ☐ Wear a travel bag strapped to your waist to conceal personal papers and money.
- ☐ Learn the city's rules, regulations, curfews and safe streets.
- ☐ Be aware of the political stability of the country, known terrorist activities and methods of evacuation.
- ☐ Keep a low profile, remain alert and use discernment about the areas you travel.
- ☐ Upgrade to a sleeping compartment for additional security during overnight train travel.

See also "Travel Warnings" on page 101.

HOME CARE

- ☐ Install deadbolt locks on all exterior doors.
- ☐ Lock all doors when the family is absent from the home and always use the alarm system.
- ☐ Plan one or two practice routes for your family to exit your home in case of fire.
- ☐ Place a locking bar on all sliding glass doors.
- ☐ Secure all ladders.
- ☐ Tell trusted neighbors and police when you are on vacation.
- ☐ Do not hide keys outside of your home.
- ☐ Check smoke detector batteries twice a year.
- ☐ Discontinue mail and newspaper deliveries when traveling.
- ☐ Install night lights, sensor lights and timers inside and outside the home. Keep flashlights accessible.
- ☐ Use baby gates and child-resistant locks.
- ☐ Purchase a fire extinguisher for your home.

PET / VETERINARIAN

Name of pet _____

Species _____ Male _____ Female _____

License # _____

Color/markings _____

_____

_____

Owner _____

Tel # 1 _____ # 2 _____

Address _____

_____

Veterinarian _____

Address _____

_____

Tel/Fax _____

Emergency information _____

Vaccination/Appointments	**Date**
_____	_____
_____	_____
_____	_____
_____	_____
_____	_____
_____	_____

Condition/Illness	**Treatment/Medication**
_____	_____
_____	_____
_____	_____

DIRECTORY OF INTERNET SITES

TRAVEL AND SAFETY

Travel Warnings http://travel.state.gov Travel and safety issues for every country of the world and US Embassy or Consulate locations.

Shoreland's Travel Health Online http://www.tripprep.com The home of travel, health and safety.

Centers for Disease Control and Prevention http://www.cdc.gov/ Frequently updated country-specific information about illnesses and immunizations. Publications, software and more.

REAL ESTATE

The International Real Estate Directory http://www.ired.com Lists thousands of real estate sites around the world, as well as general information about buying and selling real estate.

EscapeArtist http://www.escapeartist.com Country and regional guides, Embassy Pages and working overseas resources.

Rent Net http://www.rent.net/international/ International rentals.

Forward Mobility http://www.forwardmobility.com A global relocation consulting service that offers assistance with home sales/purchases and rentals overseas, as well as real estate legal considerations.

Relocation Property Services (RPS) http://www.rpsrelocation.com RPS offers numerous free resources such as school profiles, checklists for moving and real estate, articles about children and spouse concerns and relocation software. They also have a network of certified relocation service providers that offer discounted services.

Homenet http://www.centernet.com/gif/inter.htm Lists available properties (many with photos) and contact information within twenty countries. Some listings are written only in the foreign language.

DUAL CAREER RESOURCES

Career Mosaic http://www.careermosaic.com Job-hunting advice, employer profiles and links to corporations that are hiring.

101

International Staffing Consultants, Inc. http://www.iscworld.com
Recruits and selects professional and technical staff for international
jobs. No charge for submitting résumés and reviewing job openings.

Careerpath http://www.careerpath.com Combines the classifieds of six
major newspapers and carries résumé and employer/job seeker
matching services.

JobOptions http://www.joboptions.com Perform a job search, post your
résumé, sign up for E-mail job alerts and search employers.

Wall Street Journal http://careers.wsj.com Resource for those interested
in management, sales, marketing, finance and technology.

On-line Career Center http://www.occ.com A job search engine that
also offers free résumé hosting.

Job Search Sources http://www.overseasjobs.com Lists 700+ career,
job-listing and recruiter sites in 40+ countries.

EDUCATION

International Schools Services (ISS) http://www.iss.edu ISS publishes
The ISS Directory of Overseas Schools, a comprehensive guide to
primary and secondary American and international schools.

WWTeach http://members.aol.com/wwteach/Teach.htm This site can be
accessed from most browsers. Lists International Schools & Associations,
International Educators' E-mail Addresses, Virtual/ Electronic Educational
Field Trips and more.

TIPS' Guide to International Schools
http://www.iteachnet.com/Ourguideb.html In-depth listings of
international schools for 63 countries around the world. Website
addresses, E-mail addresses and statistics for each school.

European Council of International Schools (ECIS) http://www.ecis.org/
The International Schools Directory and Higher Education Institutions.

WorldWide Classroom http://www.worldwide.edu An Internet library of
over 11,000 intercultural and educational programs around the world.
The International Study Telecom Directory lists thousands of schools
worldwide. Resource for study, teaching or internships abroad.

American Community Schools (ACS) http://www.acs-england.co.uk ACS
offers a traditional American diploma or the International Baccalaureate
for students Pre-K through grade 13. Fully accredited with a flexible
curriculum that facilitates transition to schools in other countries.

FINANCES

Social Security Online http://www.ssa.gov Publications and online direct services on how to report fraud.

Internal Revenue Service http://www.irs.ustreas.gov Electronic filing of US income tax.

Money Magazine http://www.money.com Information about taxes, cost-of-living comparator, car buyer's guide and more.

DOCUMENTATION

Passport information http://travel.state.gov/passport_services.html

Visa information http://travel.state.gov/visa_services.html

The Embassy Web http://www.embpage.org The Internet Presence Provider of Choice for Embassies, Consulates and UN Missions.

NEWS

Washington Post http://www.washingtonpost.com

The Washington Times http://www.washtimes.com

Christian Science Monitor http://www.csmonitor.com

National Public Radio http://www.npr.org

BBC NEWS http://www.bbc.co.uk Offers news in English.

ORGANIZATIONS

Expat Exchange http://www.expatexchange.com An online community for people of all nationalities who are moving or living abroad connect with peers to share information and advice. Expert advice, job and resume postings, a welcome service and community newsletter.

The Web of Culture http://www.webofculture.com A wealth of information relating to cross-cultural communications. This comprehensive site informs its audience about the people and cultures of the world covering world capitals, news headlines, body language and more.

American Citizens Abroad http://www.aca.ch A non-profit organization that works for legislative and regulatory reform in the areas of citizenship, taxation, health care, Social Security, education, voting, consulates and census. Representatives are in countries around the world.

TCK World http://www.tckworld.com Resources for the parents and teachers of Third Culture Kids (TCKs) who are dealing with the many challenges of cross-cultural transitions. TCK World provides materials for cross-cultural moves, as well as culture-shock and repatriation.

Overseas Digest http://overseasdigest.com Features more than 30 of the most important government documents for Americans abroad, including taxes, social security, safety and security issues. Offers a free monthly E-mail newsletter, *Overseas Digest.*

ELDER CARE

Elder Care Industry http://www.elderindustry.com Learn more about *The Complete Eldercare Planner* and work/life presentations by author and speaker, Joy Loverde. *See also* page two in this book.

Transitions, Inc. http://www.asktransitions.com Light-hearted and fun site to educate and support those touched by the aging process.

National Academy of Elder Law Attorneys, Inc.
http://www.naela.com/naela/what is.htm Answers many basic questions about elder law, benefiting the elder and the caregiver.

OTHER RELEVANT SITES

IAMAT http://www.cybermall.co.nz/NZ/IAMAT/ International Association for Medical Assistance to Travelers provides contacts for English- and French-speaking doctors.

Multicultural Pavilion
http://curry.edschool.virginia.edu/go/multicultural This site provides resources and dialogues for educators, students and activists. It offers International Photo Galleries, Multicultural Paths (links) to other sites and more.

iAgora http://www.iagora.com Talk to people around the world about studying, traveling and working abroad. Also has destination specific information, practice languages, travel articles, European soccer, and more. Site in English, French, German and Spanish.

Windham International http://www.windhamworld.com Windham International provides cross-cultural training, homefinding, settling-in, and other services to corporations and their expatriates anywhere in the world.

Video Overseas Incorporated http://www.videooverseas.com Provides dual voltage (110/220volts) electronics and appliances and multi-system electronics. Converts existing appliances and electronics with transformers, adapters, voltage stabilizers and surge protectors.

GlobalPhone Corporation http://www.gphone.com Provides the international community with an alternative to the high cost of doing business with traditional phone companies overseas. Services include International Callback and Webcallback.

The List http://thelist.iworld.com Information to access an Internet Service Provider (ISP) by area code in the US and Canada or by country code for countries worldwide.

Expat Forum http://www.expatforum.com Human Resource E-mail discussion group, bookstore and a wealth of expat-related tips and links.

Virtual World Tours http://www.dreamscape.com/frankvad/world.html A wonderful site to learn about a new country. Over 100 city or country destinations can be reviewed. Travel related information, pictures of the cities' highlights, world maps, weather *and more.*

FOR MORE INFORMATION...

❐ Please add me to your mailing list.

❐ Send me details about publishing a customized relocation book.

❐ Send me volume pricing for the products specified.

_____

_____

_____

TO ORDER: (V/MC accepted) Dalene Bickel, Director, Publications, BR Anchor Publishing, 2044 Montrose Lane, Wilmington, NC 28405. Tel: in the United States (800) 727-7691 and from other countries (910) 256-9598, Fax: (910) 256-9579 and E-mail: branchor@inttek.net

TO CUSTOMIZE: Beverly D. Roman, Publisher, BR Anchor Publishing, 2044 Montrose Lane, Wilmington, NC 28405. Tel: (910) 256-9598, FAX: (910) 256-9579 and E-mail: BRAnchor@aol.com

BR Anchor Publishing on the web: http://www.branchor.com

MY INFORMATION

Name _____

Company _____

Address _____

_____

Postal code _____ Country _____

Tel _____ Fax _____

E-mail _____

Web site _____

Relocation needs _____

_____

About the Author

Beverly D. Roman has written twelve relocation books and writes the online monthly newsletter, *Relocation...2000*. The author is recognized and quoted as an expert in the field of relocation. Having relocated 18 times with a family of five, Beverly has a thorough understanding of what is productive and what is counter-productive to achieving relocation success.

Beverly D. Roman has been featured on CNN's "Parenting Today," ABC TV's "Home Show" and Discovery Channel's "Home Matters" with her relocation expertise. She has also contributed to major relocation publications such as *Runzheimer Reports on Relocation, Mobility, Personnel Journal, Direction, Horizons, HR Briefing* and numerous parents magazines and leading newspapers.

OTHER BOOKS BY THE AUTHOR

Moving Minus Mishaps / Moving Minus Mishaps rev. ed.

The Graduate's Handbook

"When in Rome ..."

The Insiders' Guide to Relocation

Let's Make A Move! (for small children)

ReloCenter™

¡Vamos a Mudarnos! (for small children in Spanish)

ReloCenter International

Moving Forward (for teenagers)

Let's Move Overseas (for small children)

CUSTOMS ANSWERS

PAGE NO.	COUNTRY
18	Greece
21	Iran
22	Egypt
26	Peru
27	England
28	Spain
30	Germany
32	Argentina
36	China
39	Italy
46	Austria
52	Poland
54	Colombia
57	Japan
61	Belgium
62	Norway
64	Japan
66	Turkey
87	Kenya
97	Paraguay